# The Alphabet of Love

# of Love

## A primer for the language of the heart

## Thomas G. Fiffer

Published by Christmas Lake Press 2022
www.christmaslakecreative.com

Copyright © 2022 Thomas G. Fiffer

ISBN: 978-1-7377000-5-0

Interior layout by Daiana Marchesi

# Dedication

To those whose enduring love sustains me:
My parents—may they rest in peace
My brothers and their families
My children
and my first, always and forever love—J

# Acknowledgments

The muse

Metro-North

Daiana Marchesi

Abigail Bates

All the friends and readers who have encouraged me

*Love, then, is not expended like money, for in addition to the fact that money is diminished by expenditure and love is increased, they differ in this too, that we give greater evidence of good-will towards anyone if we do not seek the return of money we have given him; whereas no one can sincerely expend love unless he tenderly insists on being repaid; for when money is received, it is so much gain to the recipient but so much loss to the donor; love, on the other hand, is not only augmented in the man who demands it back from the person he loves, even when he does not receive it, but the person who returns it actually begins to possess it only when he pays it back.*

— St. Augustine, *Epistle No. 44*

*I walk in the world to love it.*

— Mary Oliver

*"How do you spell 'love'?" — Piglet*
*"You don't spell it...you feel it." — Pooh*

— A. A. Milne

*All writing is an act of translation.*
*It turns something you see or sense*
*into something you say.*

— Maya Jasanoff

# Contents

# Prologue

When I launched my blog, Tom Aplomb, in June 2008, I was bitter. Although I had recently remarried, the wounds from my divorce and dysfunctional first marriage were fresh. After many years of silence, my quiet, reflective, writerly voice wanted to say something, but my angry, aggrieved, and vehement voice demanded to be heard, to catapult like an angry bird and smash my ex, my pain, my past life to pieces. My early posts took the form of rants—how *could* she?—or laments—how could *this* have happened to *me*? I steered clear of self-pity but made pitiful progress on the road to self-awareness and self-understanding. I was a mess, and I wanted the world to know it wasn't my fault.

Three things happened to change the blog's trajectory and alter its target.

First, a Twitter acquaintance told me I needed to use my real name if I wished to be taken seriously. I had been hiding behind a *nom de plume*, Tom Aplomb, concerned that people who knew me would see my story and devour the details of my emotional and psychological undoing. I hadn't yet watched Brené Brown's famous TED talk, and

I was as much ashamed of my life as I was outraged at its severely damaged state. I also worried that my ex would find the blog or that parents of my young children's school classmates would, to use a contemporary term, cancel me—and my sons' playdates. With trepidation, I took ownership of my truth—deciding to let the reactions fall where they may.

Second, the reactions realigned my direction. As readers related to my story and found wisdom in my words, I realized the purpose of my posts was to help others and not just heal myself. By turning my focus outward, I turned the blog from a source of self-soothing to a source of solace for those who had experienced hurt, heartbreak, harmful relationships—the hard truths of the human condition. The impact my writing was having on readers made my daily discipline (publishing each morning on my commute to Manhattan) a daily delight, a delicious weight, a labor of love.

Third, and most momentous, when my second marriage fizzled, I reconnected with my first love, after nearly twenty years of separation. One of her many gifts was my spiritual awakening. She taught me to listen with my heart and look toward heaven for the message I was meant to convey, and my writing took on a poetic quality and sacred aspect that often astonished me—and still does.

As my posts piled up, I made many attempts to organize, categorize, and synthesize them into a book.

But no framework seemed to make sense. Only when I came up with the idea for this volume—a testament to the letters of love from a lover of letters—did I realize I had been writing about love all along. And then everything made sense. So here it is, *The Alphabet of Love*.

## Love is an Art

Sit.

Silently.

Close your eyes and listen.

Let it come to you.

And it will come.

This morning I sat.

Silently.

Listening.

And I thought I heard, no, I knew I heard, the sound of breaking waves.

The sound of water ebbing and flowing, washing whitely over the rocks before receding along the sand.

The cycle of nature, repeating itself.

The cycle of endless regeneration.

And I felt something, deep in my heart.

A strengthening of the muscle.

A quickening of the beat.

A pulsating throb creating flow.

The energy of the artist at work.

Engineers build bridges.

Artists engineer change.

Artists deliver difference.

Our stock in trade is revelation.

Suddenly the phrase *be the change* made sense to me.

In the context of art.

In the context of God the creator, the ultimate artist, who spoke the world to life with words. Who created light from darkness, being from nothingness. Who brought forth what was not there before. Whose light illuminates every manuscript. Whose music speaks to every composer. Whose hand guides every chisel, brush, and pen.

Be the change.

Banish anger, bitterness, and frustration.

Send them packing.

Fill yourself with love and light.

Give of your heart and free your words.

Spill your blood onto the pages.

The blood of sacrifice.

Sail across the wine-dark sea.

Show them the struggling.

The drowning.

The sinking.

The rising again.

And break like waves upon their heads.

Touch them.

Alter them.

Leave your mark.

And make it . . .

indelible.

Creative freedom is not something you indulge.

It is a serious commitment to being yourself.

To using your brokenness to make the world a little more whole.

The most misunderstood thing about artists is that we're flaky, irresponsible, and self-indulgent.

The world of products and services, of punch clocks and process improvement, of make-work and manufacturing, of profits and five-year plans, lays down a challenge. The world asks: How dare you make art when there is *work* to be done?

Well, I speak back the artists' challenge: How dare you waste time when there is art to be made?

How dare you expend precious resources making things that don't matter?

How dare you squander ingenuity, consume creativity, and crush spirit in a vise? How dare you try to quench the fire of inspiration?

In my challenge, there is no anger.

Only wonderment.

Because those who would deny art its primacy have somehow lost their wonderment, their sense that anything at all can be wondrous, that life can be magical, surprising, and extraordinary.

Round them up, the captains of conformity, the paragons of playing it safe.

And ship them off.

Make them spend a month in the museum, a week blaring Beethoven, a day reading Dickens, a night in bed with Nabokov.

For God's sake, make them feel. Even if just for a moment.

I will not raise my children to be cogs, to be cut and shaped and filed and smoothed for someone else's purpose.

I hereby and henceforth set them free.

Free to follow their own compass and set their own course.

Free to breathe fire, to inflame the world with their genius.

Free to leave their own indelible marks.

Free to be artists.

Free to be the change.

# Love is a Blessing

Blessings come in many forms.

Blessings come from families who set aside differences, welcome back, and support.

Blessings come from friends who move past old hurts, reconnect, and forgive.

Blessings come from colleagues who, when we're going through a rough period, pick up the slack.

Blessings come from strangers who hold open a door, point out something we just dropped, or simply smile.

Blessings come from children, who speak blessings all day long, which we only hear if we listen.

Blessings come from ourselves, when we open our hearts, share our gifts freely, and treat others with dignity and grace.

As I hold this book in my hands, I feel especially blessed.

I feel blessed to have been given the words.

I feel blessed by the muse who is my inspiration.

And I feel blessed to be at a place in my life, unbound from all that's held me back, where I can create, inspire, and share.

Blessings abound.

Blessings are everywhere.

Blessings are universal and infinite and often unexpected.

Blessings ultimately all flow from the same source, because they flow through us, not from us, when we bless.

Who will you bless today?

## Love is a Bond

A bond is like a house, a shared home in which two spirits dwell.

A bond is more than a connection that binds us.

A bond is a space of connection we inhabit.

A sacred space two people honor.

A consistently respectful way of relating.

The feeling of home we create through loving interaction.

The quality of light that flows from loving companionship.

The fresh scent of the air flowing in through the open window.

The warm glow of the hearth fire.

The smell of the shared meal cooking.

The sweet taste of a shared chalice.

The security of closing our eyes, knowing where our bond-mate is, knowing we can lean back without fear . . . and fall into those waiting arms.

# Love is Compassion

This morning, in my sacred space, I felt the peace again.

More intensely than before.

Like falling down a deep hole and being raised up at the same time.

I spent the weekend writing, walking, swimming in the Sound.

I did my work, and when I finished my work, I did what I wanted.

I did the things that make me happy.

I enjoyed beauty, captured beauty, shared beauty.

I looked up at the sky and watched the light change.

I listened to the sound of the waves.

I waited patiently, as late afternoon fell softly into evening, to add more pink beauties to my catalog of clouds.

And this morning, I woke early and enjoyed the sunrise, something I hadn't done in well over a year.

The first thing I saw, as I walked the gentle, curving expanse of Compo Beach, was the moon.

The moon reminded me that the moment before sunrise is still night. That daybreak breaks through the barrier separating dark and light.

I have trained my eyes to notice the subtle changes in color that sculpt the texture of the morning sky. Blue deepening into purple then brightening into pink.

And I felt my spirit leaping as I neared the jetty at the end of the beach that stretches out into the sea.

From the jetty, I witnessed a red glow growing up from then over the trees as the big ball of sun began to rise.

I felt the miracle of soul flight, and breathed in the beauty of rising, just as a bird took off.

The peace flowed down through the warming light, and I felt the sun on the back of my neck—a welcome friend.

We rarely think of peace as intense, but I believe peace is energy channeled properly, energy harnessed for good, action aligned with purpose and call.

The power of this peace was volcanic.

Back at home, I experienced the peace differently than at the beach.

There was no sun to look at, only the leaves rustling gently in the wind outside my window.

What I felt sitting there was the source of the peace.

I already knew where it comes from.

But what generates it? What makes it flow? What is it about God's presence that brings peace to the world?

I *heard* the word beneficence—the quality of being kind and charitable.

But I *felt* the word compassion, felt the compassion itself, the immense sorrow He holds for our suffering, the infinite care in His heart.

And I knew that while sunrise—and sunset—are His daily treats for us, serving as both symbols and reminders of His magnificence, the compassion He extends to all of us is His ultimate gift.

## Love is Devotion

I had only a moment to sit in my space this morning.

But I was determined.

Determined to give that moment . . . to God.

And I heard the word devotion.

Just one word.

That was all.

A hard word.

Lovely and hard all in one.

Bittersweet and both/and.

Most words that start with d are negative.

I'm sure you can name a few.

There are the three ds on which auction houses depend for most of their business: debt, divorce, and death.

There are disdain, derision, and divisiveness.

Dastardly and devious.

Dark and dank.

Dereliction, desecration, and damnation.

Demonization.

Destruction.

And that sad word, depressed.

But then there is devotion.

A happy word if you embrace it, if you devote yourself willingly and with love.

We often encounter the word devoted after a person's life is over.

A devoted father or husband, mother or wife.

Devotion describes the way one person went about loving and caring for another.

Present, committed, and ever faithful, right up to the end.

We hear about it after death, but devotion happens while life is being lived.

The roots of devotion lie in the Latin *devotionem*, a "noun of action" meaning "to dedicate by a vow, sacrifice oneself, promise solemnly." The stem *devovere* breaks into *de*—down, away—and *vovere*—vow.

Devotion is not a state of mind or being but the action of devoting, the constant and consistent faith in the other that fosters forbearance and forgiveness.

I do not believe the sacrifice of devotion means giving up everything you care about, letting your life dissipate, or allowing your sacred self to be absorbed and consumed by another person. That is not devotion at all, but a form of codependence—an unhealthy abdication of your own purpose and call.

I also do not believe devotion exists in the conceptual vacuum, because in practice, unless we are up for sainthood, we find it impossible to devote ourselves when the other person refuses or is unable to devote him or herself back. The vow of devotion is a mutual agreement between two people and generally does not withstand repeated betrayals or significant breaches of trust.

But sometimes it can.

Perhaps, if we had God's patience . . .

Devotion is not love, but devotion flows from love.

Devotion is the action love engenders.

Devotion is the oxygen in love's breath.

Devotion is calling even when the other person is angry, especially when the other person is angry.

Devotion is answering, even when you yourself are mad.

Devotion is working the magic of creating memories, summoning the mettle to deal with the mess, the marvel of committing wholeheartedly to another's goals and dreams.

Devotion is replacing a bitter aftertaste with the memory of something sweet.

Devotion is what gets us through when nothing else can.

Devotion is trudging into the garden during the rainstorm, covering the tender shoots, protecting the plants to ensure the harvest, because we reap not merely what we sow but also what we devote ourselves to growing.

Devotion takes work, and devotion, in its highest form, is pure joy.

## Love is Eternal

Love is forever.

Abuse has a half-life.

Love is eternal.

Abuse is perpetual.

Love is consistent.

Abuse is predictable.

Love is steadfast.

Abuse is relentless.

Love is humble.

Abuse is humiliating.

Love is tender.

Abuse is raw.

Love is purposeful.

Abuse is premeditated.

Love is sacred.

Abuse is sanctimonious.

Love is hard.

Abuse is hardened.

Love is rudimentary

Abuse is crude.

Love is electric.

Abuse is shocking.

Love is catalytic.

Abuse is cataclysmic.

Love is dependable.

Abuse is dependent.

Love is determined.

Abuse is determining.

Love is surrender

Abuse is submission.

Love is free.

Abuse is rootless.

Love is encompassing.

Abuse is imprisoning.

Love is everywhere.

Abuse is endemic.

Love is God.

Abuse is Godless.

Love is a discipline.

Abuse is a choice.

# Love is Faith

The other day, I found myself revisiting an earlier post called Reconditioning.

I headlined it with a Kodachrome-style picture of a six or seven-year-old girl—about to jump off a high dive—with a look of frightened excitement on her face.

The girl is simultaneously enthralled with the thrill of making the leap and scared that she will fall or fail, but her poised legs, raised arms, and clenched fists reveal her determination: I have come this far; I am going to do it; there is no turning back.

Reconditioning is about how we're conditioned from birth to admire risk takers—achievers who realize their dreams, celebrities who make it against the odds, heroes who set aside their fear to save lives or brave new worlds, visionaries who change the world through perseverance—and also constantly admonished to avoid risk, to be prudent and careful, to take the proven path and play it safe.

At the core of this conundrum is trust.

If our parents, teachers, mentors, and other influencers don't trust us to overcome obstacles and push through to a life of fulfillment and meaning, we find it difficult to trust ourselves. We're told—or shown by the withholding of trust—that all that glory, all that satisfaction of self-actualization, all that joy of hitting our mark, that's for other people. You probably won't make it if you try that, so just be happy with a decent job, a mortgage—or two—the absence of need, and the pervasive smell of mediocrity every time you breathe. Really, it's OK. I had to give up my dreams, too, so you might as well join the club. And honestly, who the hell do you think you are to pursue yours?

The opposite of encouragement is discouragement—a dis—stripping us of the courage to go for it.

Lately, I've been learning to trust more.

To trust in myself and my abilities.

To be more confident—again.

And to draw from a new source of confidence . . .

To trust in God.

To have faith.

To hand things over to Him.

To walk out onto the high dive and trust that if I leap, He will catch me, in those big broad hands of His.

This isn't easy for a self-reliant person raised as a secular Jew.

It isn't easy at all.

The trust of faith is a shift that must become a practice—like aplomb—to be sustained.

But trust is my new venture.

And while venture, citing Etymology Online, means "to risk the loss of something," for an implied reward or better outcome, when you've lost as much as I have, there is not much left but to venture forth and trust. And trusting venture, I found it derives from adventure, which means both "that which happens by chance, fortune, luck," and "a wonder, a miracle; accounts of marvelous things."

To venture is to trust that miracles and marvelous things will happen when we take a chance and risk loss.

The truth is, we risk loss every time we give. But when we give from the heart, when we give to nurture and nourish others and to feed our dreams and theirs, when we give to make our own and others' gardens grow, when we invest our love, our kindness, our generosity, and ultimately our trust, in people we love, respect, and admire, and in activities that support, sustain, and enrich, we become wealthy beyond measure.

So, nothing ventured, nothing gained.

Here goes . . .

\* \* \*

Looking out the bedroom window of my mother's lakefront apartment in Chicago at night, I noticed the red guide lights atop the Aon Center, known during my childhood as the Standard Oil Building.

The building looks like a smaller version of one of the now-vanished twin towers, and it is high enough to require the protective nighttime lights that make it visible from a distance and, in theory, prevent planes from crashing into it.

I noticed the configuration of the guide lights, three on each corner of the building, a trinity if you will.

And I noticed something else. In each group of three lights, the two on the outside remained on, while the light in the middle flashed rhythmically—on and off, on and off.

I thought about that middle light.

When it flashed off, it was still there. I just couldn't see it.

Sometimes, I could see the middle light, and sometimes I couldn't.

But whether I could see it or not, it was still there.

So I thought about the light we can't always see.

The light that is always there, whether we see it or whether we don't.

I thought about how, if that light is to guide us, we must have faith in the darkness, faith during the times when we can't see the light.

We must have faith in the constancy of that light's presence and understand it is not the light that is inconstant but our ability to see it that flashes on and off, on and off.

During the day, none of the lights are visible.

But at night, the two lights on either side of the middle one serve as witnesses, a testament to its presence and an indication of its position.

And as I fell asleep under the blinking glow of the guide lights, I felt my eyes opening even as they closed.

## Love is Forever

Lately, I've been thinking about time.

Here, we measure it one way.

Up there, it's measured differently.

Up there, it isn't measured at all.

A lifetime, when we begin it, seems like an eternity.

But eternity is a concept we cannot grasp.

Eternity slips through our fingers, like every passing day.

Forever in this world means until we leave this world.

But forever in the world of spirit has nothing to do with leaving.

Forever in the world of spirit is an endless span of time.

Forever in the world of spirit is not time at all.

There, forever encompasses past, present, and future, and in doing so ignores these inadequate terms we use to describe which way we're turning at any given time.

In a world where we strive to measure everything, forever is forgotten, because it does not fit onto a yardstick, round out a balance sheet, or encompass the scope of an empire. Forever is given short shrift in favor of the short term.

The closest we can come to forever in this world is to see that there is no time and there is always time, to feel no loss as what we call time ticks away, to experience the endless calming flow of being, the rhythm of sun and moon, the balance of light and darkness, the wonder of days without numbers, the miracle of wave after wave lapping peacefully over the glistening sand.

# Love is Free

The fireflies are back.

I am grateful that they return every summer, their phosphorescent flashes punctuating the slow, rhythmic progression of dusk.

Just before darkness falls, my yard comes alive with stabs of yellow-green brightness, here, there, evanescent and repetitive, consistently unpredictable, filling my heart with anticipatory pleasure.

Yes, you can catch them, cup your hands around their tiny, suspended bodies, jar them, scrutinize them to reveal the secret of their glow. But you cannot capture their magic. It doesn't belong to you.

If you cage love or beauty, try to steal and possess its light, it will flicker, fade, and die.

But you can live by its light, thrive in the shine, if you abide the cycle of capture and release.

Respect that fireflies are visitors, gracing you with their presence. They don't have to come.

Connect with their unique gift, their freedom to appear and disappear as they alternatively highlight the air and meld with the dark.

Absorb their beauty, feel it deeply, hold it lightly, as it flows through you.

Appreciate their magic, as it comes close, dips into the distance, then returns, always in a slightly different spot.

I am grateful for fireflies, ever so grateful.

# Love is Generosity

I just read that Sasha Dichter is rebooting Valentine's Day 2011 as Generosity Day.

This is a stunning idea.

Besides moving away from the gross and wasteful materialism, the unrealistic expectations, the dashed hopes and inevitable disappointment, and the immense depths of loneliness that the way our culture chooses to promote and celebrate Cupid's birthday make anyone who is not with someone else feel, Dichter's concept reminds us that generosity is a key, if not the key component of love.

Here's my take on the importance of generosity.

When we feel abundance, it is easy to be generous. Giving doesn't drain our resources, and we can afford to break off small parts of ourselves and give them to others. We know there is more where those parts came from, because we are growing, and there is no real risk of damage to ourselves.

When we feel pinched, depleted, depressed, and cheated of life's good stuff, it is hard to be generous, or to give at all. Our emptiness swallows us. We feel we have nothing to give, and that even if we tried, no one would appreciate our efforts. It's all worthless. I'm worthless. What's the point?

When we reach this point, a low point for the self, and a high point for the part of us that's intent on self-sabotage, we turn inward, and often start ripping ourselves apart before we can begin to put ourselves back together.

This is precisely the moment when it is critical to turn outward, to take the focus off ourselves and our problems, no matter how severe, and try to reach out, to connect with others, to contribute something meaningful for them, even if that contribution is just a smile. That may be all we're capable of, but doing it puts us on the road to recovery and redemption.

It's not so much that we get some perspective on our situation by hearing about someone else's (perhaps learning that what we're going through is not as terrible as someone else's ordeal). It's more that we stop listening to the voice inside that's laden with negativity because we're suddenly listening to, engaged with, and offering something to someone else, someone in need, someone who will benefit from even the most modest gesture we can make. The power of doing this cannot be underestimated.

In a related post, Susan Piver inspires us to make Valentine's Day a day of love by walking us through the steps of how to expand our definition of love from romantic feelings for one person to encompass "all the love we have ever felt in our lives." She gives us a clear sense of direction, no matter where love has taken us, with the following three lines:

"If you are in a relationship, make today all about him or her."

"If you aren't in a relationship, make every being you encounter today into a loved one."

"And if your heart is broken, you're in the best shape of all for a day of love because all you have is love."

Following these is a list of seven simple ways to be generous, ways to give gifts that, while small in size, have the potential for enormous impact. When you do these things, and other things like them, you may never know how much you have helped someone. But the person you helped will know, and that person will never forget.

So as the big day approaches, set your mind—and your heart—at ease. You don't have to buy into the hoopla—or buy anyone anything. Like any other day, it's what you make of it.

* * *

How can you be generous when you feel you have nothing?

As a seeker of balance I frequently find myself leaning into ambiguity.

Maintaining poise by embracing uncertainty and accepting a world of both/and.

And savoring the sweet, delicious center of life instead of nibbling with rigid restraint at one hard edge or the other.

I find that not only enlightenment but also the bright colors of joy live not at either strictly-defined end but in the ever-morphing middle of the spectrum.

Take, for example, the art of generous giving.

There is the "selfless" giving of martyrdom that results in damaging self-sacrifice and engenders bitter resentment.

But this sort of giving is not generous, because it exacts a steep price from the recipient. Debt service is constantly demanded but by definition impossible to repay.

"I do everything for you and this is the thanks I get."

The giver doesn't want you to *have*, he wants you to *owe*.

Then there is the "self-indulgent" giving, the endless overextending intended to buy the recipient's loyalty and affection.

The flaw here is that the giver gives only because he wants something and fails to understand the true value of loyalty and affection.

That these priceless presents are not bought but won.

That these magnificent jewels are mined with massive effort, cut with consistent commitment, and polished with persistent care and attention.

Mined, not "mine."

The balance is found in between.

In giving for the joy of giving, straight from the heart.

In giving because you want the recipient to enjoy.

Because you derive enjoyment from his enjoyment.

Because making her happy makes you happy, too.

The balance resides in the center, in the core of the shining diamond, in the brilliant, flawless light of love.

# Love is Happiness

*When we are no longer able to change a situation, we are challenged to change ourselves.*
— Viktor Frankl, *Man's Search for Meaning*

*And I ain't the Lord, no I'm just a fool*
*Learning loving somebody don't make them love you*
— Jack Johnson, *Sitting, Wishing, Waiting*

A while back I wrote a Facebook status that I knew would turn into an article for *The Good Men Project*.

When we remain in an unhealthy relationship, we believe we are waiting for our partner to change. In truth, we are waiting for ourselves to change, a process that often takes longer than we expect.

It took me 15 years to figure this out—much longer than I expected—and another seven to connect it with happiness, and I believe this fundamental misconception is responsible for millions of unhappy relationships—both personal and professional—and perhaps billions of unhappy people. Yes, billions.

So here's the nut: Happy people don't try to change other people or wait for them to change. They work on themselves.

It's stunningly simple.

But stunningly difficult to embrace.

Why?

Because we tend to believe that happy people are lucky and unhappy people aren't. It's easier to believe that, more comfortable to believe that, than to admit that happiness is a choice, or more accurately, the result of a series of choices.

Put another way, it's easier to answer the question, "Why am I so unlucky?" than "Why am I so unhappy?" The second question requires deep introspection and achieving self-awareness, while the first can only be acknowledged as rhetorical or answered with a statement that avoids personal accountability (e.g., "Because God hates me"), because luck by definition is beyond our control.

In *Thinking, Fast and Slow*, Daniel Kahneman's groundbreaking exploration of intuitive and deliberate thinking, he explains the phenomenon of replacing one question with another: "When faced with a difficult question, we often answer an easier one instead, usually without noticing the substitution."

Happy people may appear not to be doing any work to be happy. It just seems to flow for them. But happy people always return the focus to the more difficult question, the one with an answer that in all likelihood requires hard work on the self, while their unhappier counterparts default to the belief—and false sense of relief—that others need to change, a belief that is fatal to their pursuit of peace and contentment. The sooner we learn that people only change when they want to, at their own rate, on their own schedule, the sooner we can get busy on ourselves. Personal growth can be encouraged from without but can only occur from within.

In conjunction with the flawed belief that others must change first, we also put too much faith in our power to influence others, setting ourselves up for crushing disappointment—and potentially paralyzing depression—when we fail in our futile attempts to change them. This often leads to our stepping it up (because we've been trained never to quit and to keep trying harder) and trying to force change through threats and manipulation. Can you think of a greater recipe for unhappiness than that? Except perhaps engaging in an endless, pointless struggle?

Happy people are not the shiny, lucky, blessed ones to whom nothing bad ever seems to happen. They're the ones who handle the bad stuff in stride.

And it's not that happy people don't have losses. They do, just like the rest of us. But they act faster to cut them and move on.

So the next time you're wondering, ask yourself, "Where am I focusing my change energy? On others? Or on myself?"

The answer will tell you everything you need to know about being happy.

# Love is Heart

The heart is a living rock.

A most miraculous thing.

Steady and steadfast.

Yet able to assume any tempo and rhythm.

Adamant in love.

Yet soft and glowing in compassion.

A fixed star.

A constant, pulsing beacon.

Our life force.

The driving force of love.

The heart moves us.

We do not move the heart.

The heart creates flow, and the beat sustains it.

And when two hearts beat as one, a transformative exchange occurs, a mutual refreshing that is nothing short of magical.

The heart's love is an elixir.

A kind of liquid oxygen.

Hope in a bottle.

The form faith would take if faith could take a physical form.

When life seals us in a cold, dark, and airless cave—the heart's love is warmth and light and breath.

When life sinks us to the bottom of the ocean—the heart's love lifts us to the surface.

And when we reach the point on our journey when we can go no further, when we know another step will cause us to stumble and collapse—the heart's love takes our hand, slips a shoulder under our bent frame, and says, *lean on me. I will support you. I will stay with you and walk you home.*

Yes, the heart speaks.

But heart words are felt, not heard.

Because heart words are actions.

Word and deed in one.

Our hearts are given to us by God.

And for God, words and actions are one and the same.

God *said* let there be light, and there *was* light.

The Hebrew word for light, אור, translates as "ohr."

And though the corresponding word in English has no literal connection, the implied irony is impossible to ignore.

Not words or action, but both embodied in the same word.

His Word.

His Light.

"Words," as Elie Wiesel wrote, "can sometimes, in moments of grace, attain the quality of deeds."

Indeed. When the heart speaks, they can.

# Love is Inner Peace

We all seek love.

Some search for it desperately.

But love is everywhere around us.

Everywhere.

When we find love, it is because love comes to us.

Love comes a-knocking.

Because we've finally let love know where we live.

Finally cleared the air, cleansed our souls, and created an atmosphere in which love can breathe.

Love needs a spark to start.

It does.

But fire needs air to survive.

And in an airless room, no amount of matches or fuel will keep the fire burning.

I believe the air love thrives on is I.P.

Inner Peace.

Chaos, turmoil, anxiety, and dissatisfaction flake off the charred remains of old burnt-out fires like particles of soot and ash, fouling the air with toxic dust.

Disappointment, indifference, cynicism, and bitterness suck out the oxygen, thinning the air to uselessness.

And self-loathing chokes off the flow of air entirely.

When the fire goes out, we're left shivering with that most devastating of all love-killers—coldness.

Inner peace is the ultimate air supply.

A perpetual pump with a line to the source: God's eternal, endless, forgiving love.

And the peace that flows from knowing Him.

You may not find love on the Internet, despite the ubiquitous offers.

But love does have an IP address.

Love makes its home in hearts filled with inner peace.

# Love is Joy

Joy is a feeling we live to experience—and experience to live.

The elation of floating on top of the world.

Enveloped in a bubble of happy abandon.

We feel it when we fall in love…

When someone surprises us with an act of kindness…

When we see our children safe and happy…

When we've made something original and full of meaning.

Joy is rare and infrequent for many.

A fortunate accident?

An undeserved bounty?

Fate smiling for one perfect moment before the inevitable dark storm returns?

Joy can be slippery and hard to hold onto.

We lament that others seem to have more.

When we seek joy, it eludes us.

When we run after it, joy runs away.

We can't get enough yet never seem to have enough.

What seems so simple is frustratingly mysterious.

The trick is to realize we already have joy.

That joy is already inside.

Living in our own hearts, waiting to be shared.

Spread like soft butter across bread.

Sprinkled like magic dust on everyone we meet.

Joy is not what we receive but what we offer.

Joy flows from giving, from the opening of a generous heart.

We *create* joyful moments—sometimes with intention.

But often by letting go and allowing joy to unfold.

The roots of joy go back to the Middle Irish *guaire*, or noble.

So joy resides in nobility.

Not the nobility of human bloodlines.

There is no such thing.

But the nobility of being God's child.

The nobility we all share.

The nobility of being descended from the King.

## Love is Kindness

I feel blessed that the marvels of words continue to unfold for me.

This morning on the train, a woman, just seated, turned to her friend who was standing and looked at her with kind concern. The friend smiled. "It's OK. There are more seats in the back."

A moment of kindness, assuaging her friend's guilt.

So I turned to the word.

Kind.

If I had more time, I would go into the origins, the roots. Each of these posts, these explorations, is the starting point for a longer explanation.

For now, I will explore the double meaning, the two meanings associated with the same sound.

One meaning of kind is type, which establishes differentiation.

The other meaning, benevolent, loving, generous, considerate, establishes connection.

Differentiation and connection, linked together.

When we are kind to people, to those who are different from us, we connect with them.

It's easy to connect through sameness. The trick is to see the sameness to us in the differences.

That is not easy.

It is a radical concept that requires a deep openness, and the ability to let a different kind of wisdom flow up from the feeling heart and supersede the thinking mind.

Try, for a moment, to feel the spirit that unites us, that lives in all the different kinds of people, even those you may be hasty to judge or condemn.

Don't think about it.

Feel it.

Then feel what can become possible.

Differences start to melt away.

Entrenched warriors lay down their arms, then open their arms in a gesture of kindness, as if to say, you are me, and I am you. We are different and the same.

Intractable conflicts, irretrievable breakdowns, unresolvable differences, move towards reconciliation.

And peace becomes more than a distant dream.

# Love is Liminal

As the saying goes, a picture is worth a thousand words. In this case, however, a picture serves to inspire the words (though perhaps not quite a thousand) rather than as a substitute for them. Seeing the leaves of a tree in transition from vivid green to reddish gold, and pondering their pending detachment and descent, turned my thoughts to the seasons of change of which, unlike the four we associate with weather, number only three. I will call them static state, liminal state, and new static state—hardly a sexy set of terms, but sufficient for the purpose they serve.

It's the liminal (or threshold) state that I find most fascinating. There's not much to say about the other two. As I looked at the tree, words came to me: "betwixt and between," a dated phrase for being conflicted, unable to choose between two competing or radically opposed options.

We all know what between means, but contemplating its companion, betwixt, inspired intense curiosity; like learning someone you've known all your life has an identical twin you've never met. Was betwixt merely between with a twist (or twixt)? I had to see.

I've always been enchanted with etymology (the origin of words), and betwixt did not disappoint. What caught my eye in the etymological entry was the phrase "in the space that separates." The word "space" sits in the exact middle of the five-word phrase, literally separating the words on either side and establishing betwixt (and its sibling between) as a space with borders of its own, not just a line.

The implication here is that change, no matter how sudden it seems, occurs in stages, that moving from one state to another includes a *crossing over* into the between space, a space where, for a moment or measure of time, the thing (or person) changing is neither here nor there, neither vivid green nor reddish gold, neither dead nor alive.

When someone cannot process change, such as the intense grief of losing a loved one or the intense shock of severe trauma, we say they are "beside themselves," suggesting they are in this between space—no longer the same person they were but not yet the changed person they are about to be.

Trauma survivors often describe the experience of leaving their bodies during trauma, standing to the side or floating above, watching what is happening to them with an odd sense of detachment—because the terrible thing can't be happening to them and must be happening to someone else.

While trauma pushes us into the dark side of the liminal state, the act of creative expression pulls us into the light—a shimmering space where anything is possible— because our imagination has no boundaries or limits. The art we create in this space changes us, often inducing feelings of surprise ("I didn't know I had that in me," or "Where in the hell did that come from?"), familiarity ("I had forgotten that image or experience"), gratitude for the muse's visit, or simply wonder.

Similarly, our art changes those who encounter it, sometimes temporarily, sometimes permanently. Think of how many great people's paths were altered by something they saw, heard, or read. Inspiration is the catalyst that sends us into the liminal space, where we are free to engage, even indulge our imagination and create something original, valuable, transformative.

Seeing the tree and associating it with the phrase "betwixt and between" brought me into the space where I could write the words here, releasing creative energy that would have otherwise remained stored in my brain.

I suppose the ultimate liminal space is the shoreline, along with its companion, the horizon. On the beach, where solid land meets liquid sea, the waves are in a constant state of motion. You take them in their

entirety, neither coming nor going but endlessly
lapping, defining and erasing the space that separates, a
space that exists as the absence of water as much as the
presence of land.

The horizon is different, and yet the same. It seems
to be a specific, measurable distance away, but that
distance grows as fast as we cover it, suspending us in
infinite travel, our destination eluding us because it is
not a destination, only the space that separates what
we can from what we cannot see. The very same space
where imagination hovers, vibrating with magic, not
an end but a means to an end, not a distant continent
we reach and conquer, but a kingdom of air we inhabit
through the act of giving chase.

# Love is Listening

I'm a storyteller. And a teacher. So it's time I started teaching with stories.

Here's one about listening.

Two men are talking to each other in a noisy bar. Or in a totally quiet room. It doesn't matter which.

One says to the other, "My wife is a dog." Those are his spoken words. His unspoken words: everything about my life is her fault. My sucky job, my weight problem, our intractable children, my lack of energy for my life.

Either because of the noise of the bar, or because of the silence of the quiet room, the other man hears something slightly different.

He hears, "My life as a dog." Those are the words he hears coming from the other man's mouth, not the other ones. The unspoken words: everything about my life is my responsibility. If I don't stand up, howl, and bark like crazy, I'm not going to get fed. Because the person I'm with is not my owner. She's not responsible for feeding me. I'm responsible for feeding myself. And by the way, I'm actually a human, masquerading as a dog, because I'm afraid to show, to be my true self, afraid my howl and bark will be offensive to someone, and I think that living under all this fur will somehow keep me warm.

Yes, that's what the other man heard. Because he listened. Over the noise of the bar. Or in the quiet room, over the noise of his own voice, his own ego, his own needs. He was fully present in the moment of the other man's words, and so he heard what the other man actually said.

So often, we misspeak, use the wrong words, but only slightly wrong ones, to describe how we're feeling. We use words that are so close, because inside, unconsciously, we want the person we're speaking with to hear us, to hear the other words, to pick up on our silent signals. Once in a while, we are fortunate enough to converse with a trained listener—a therapist, a partner, a child (children, by the way, are awesomely good at hearing this stuff, have you noticed?), a friend.

And we get heard.

And when the trained listener speaks back to us the words we actually meant to say, those words get reflected right back at us. In your face means you are seeing your true face in the mirror. Possibly for the first time.

If we're not with a trained listener, the words we choose, the words whose sounds are so close to the words we mean, float out instantly, at light speed, and travel an infinite distance away from what we mean. And the darkness that separates the words we speak from the words we mean is why we associate such negative feelings with blackness, with night, with absence and nothingness. All those feelings are substitutes for disconnection. When you disconnect, pull the plug, everything goes . . . dark.

A trained listener is like a light, a beacon, a star. He or she can light the way to our listening to the voice inside ourselves, the one that speaks the words we mean, which are not always the words we say. Then we can finally speak freely and share our own light with the world.

Do you have a trained listener in your life? If not, one of your quests must be to find one. For when you do, you will be several steps closer to leading a life of happiness and fulfillment.

Go find your trained listener, please, and do it soon. The sooner the better.

Your trained listener might even be a dog, if you can say to your dog the things you can't say to yourself. Because dogs can hear things we can't, right?

# Love is Magic

What is magic?

Magic, in the literal sense of what a magician does, occurs when a skilled illusionist performs acts of dexterity that delight us because they appear to transcend the laws of physics and rules of logic that we believe with certainty constrain the world we know.

Even though we are consciously aware the magician's acts are illusions—dependent for their success on what we don't see because we're not looking for it—we suspend our disbelief and eagerly allow ourselves to be transported into a world we don't know, a world where anything is possible.

But there is a different sort of magic, the kind we experience in our lives when something special and unexpected happens, when someone or something we encounter opens a door, shifts our perspective, or changes us for the better.

Yesterday, I saw a wonderful (as in full of wonder) photograph by Abigail Harenberg, a Chicago-based wedding photographer who graciously shares her art with the public on Instagram and Flickr. Her caption, *Do you believe in magic?*, inspired this post. What struck me as I got in touch with why Abby's photograph moved me was that while the photograph itself is an illusion—we know there aren't really colored lights in that sky—the feelings of delight, wonder, awe, inspiration, and elevation that her image filled me with were *real*.

So, to answer Abby's question, I do believe in magic.

I believe in the magic that happens when a person shares her art and asks for nothing in return.

I believe in the magic that happens when someone gives you an unexpected compliment that makes your whole day.

I believe in the magic that occurs when one person believes in another person against all odds and the advice of people who think they know.

I believe in the magic that happens when a frightened person reveals a secret to the world and in doing so takes away the power of that secret.

I believe in the magic that happens when someone reaches out and someone reaches back.

I believe in the magic that occurs when we happen on a book, a piece of music, a painting, a structure, a photograph, or a tree that brings forth feelings from deep inside us, feelings we didn't know we had. This different sort of magic delights us because it does transcend the laws of what I'll call social physics and the logic of defensiveness that tells us to conform, to keep everything in, to share only if the deal is fair and we're ensured of getting something back, to live only to survive and protect ourselves. And when this different sort of magic occurs, like the magician's illusions it transports us into the world we don't know, the world we didn't see because we weren't looking for it, a magical, wonderful world where anything is indeed possible.

* * *

A while back, I wrote a post about magic, inspired by an Abby Harenberg photograph. I felt as I wrote then, and I feel now as I write this, that we do live in a world where anything is possible. Coincidentally, Seth Godin's one-sentence post this morning struck the same note, the one just past the highest key on the piano, the one your finger reaches for on the string of your imagination: anything *is* possible.

There are people who make magic in this world, and you know who they are. They are artists, writers, photographers, directors, creators, chefs and bartenders, performers of all kinds. They inspire and delight.

Sometimes they make their own magic in the form of unique expression they release from their souls, overcoming their fears and sharing original ideas, images, sounds, tastes, stories, ways of being. And sometimes they channel the magic of others, of the ancients, enlivening it with their own special spark.

Making magic can be complicated, but it doesn't have to be. All it requires is effort and being open to possibility. Really, that's all there is to it.

Here's an example.

Last night, I visited the Rose Bar in Manhattan's Gramercy Park Hotel. I had been there before, always sitting in the small bar area near the entrance. But it was raining, and it was cold, and I was seeking warmth and refuge, so I headed into the back room with the feeling there might be a fireplace. There was. And it was filled with a roaring wood fire. A giant stone mantel surrounded the hearth, and atop the mantel were dozens of candles.

After a while, the fire began to die down, and as it did, a man came out with an armful of logs, pulled back the screen, and stoked the fire, giving everyone the bright gift of flame again. His work done, he quietly disappeared.

And then, another man came out with a stepladder. And he proceeded to light every single one of the candles atop the mantel. Then he, too, disappeared into the recesses of the bar.

Simple.

Stunning.

Special.

I could have stayed all night.

So here's the thing.

How many times have you looked longingly at a disused fireplace—real or metaphorical—or felt the cold abandonment of candles begging to be lit?

All it takes is a little magic to light someone up, to set the world on fire.

Can you find a little magic in yourself today? Can you? I think you can.

And when you do, share your magic with someone else. Someone who needs it.

Because we all need magic.

## Love is Natural

Last night I was walking through Grand Central Terminal, in the heart of New York City.

I didn't notice the last-minute shoppers scurrying, buying flowers or chocolates or wine.

I came in through the door, checked the screen for my departure track, and started down the ramp towards the main hall.

At the top of the ramp, a man stood, headphones in ears, talking to someone on his phone. I only caught the last part of his sentence: ". . . that doesn't mean I'm going to love you tomorrow morning."

Was this the height of cynicism, the lonely, icy peak?

Or a cruel joke, intended for his intended?

He sounded serious, and I wondered if the words I hadn't heard, the words that preceded, were something like "I can say I love you, but . . ."

Perhaps the person he was speaking with had asked for a proof of love? Demanded an oral lozenge, a sip of relief, those three words that soothe our hearts the way the pink Pepto-Bismol used to ooze down over an irritated stomach in the old commercial, working wonders but curing nothing, lasting only until the next ache begins.

Love shown, love in action, is love unspoken.

Love is loving.

Love is sharing without reserve.

Love is giving and love is forgiving.

Love is gratitude.

Love is peace.

Love is a moment.

Love is forever.

And love is knowing, without being asked, the right thing, the loving thing, to say and do.

I got on my train, rode home, drove to the barbecue place, and picked up my boys, who were having dinner there with their mother and her friend. It wasn't supposed to be my night with them. But my older son had asked if I could take him and his brother for an extra night, "Pleeeease?!?"

I was supposed to have a coaching session with a client.

And I had another chapter of my novel to write.

I had traveled on Monday, getting home late, and was still tired from Saturday's snow shoveling extravaganza.

It was not the best night to take my boys.

But I knew it was the right night.

And then the blessings came.

My older son finished his homework before moving on to his games, taking all the pressure off me to ensure he got it done.

Both boys played while I wrote.

And my client was as eager as I was to reschedule.

As I got my younger son to bed, he made me set his alarm earlier, so he could get up and make 20 valentines for his class.

At 6:20 sharp, he came into my bedroom, wrapped in his white blanket, and crawled under the covers with me. He was alert and not tired, as he often is on other mornings, and after a few minutes of snuggling, he was ready to get to work.

"Do you want to start in a few minutes?"

"How about now?"

"OK."

We went into the living room, found the red paper and markers, cut five sheets into fourths, and he started drawing hearts on them and writing messages. "U R . . . Dad, how do you spell beautiful?" He also wanted to make cards for his brother, me, his mother, and her boyfriend. "But I don't want to make one about romantic love for my brother."

"Smart boy," I said.

My favorite of all was LOL, which he told me meant Lots of Love, even though he knew what the letters usually stood for.

Later, big brother awoke in the best mood and thanked me over and over for the extra time. Before he went to sleep, I had apologized for being glued to my computer, writing, and not spending much time with him. He smiled and said, "Dad, just your presence is enough for me."

My heart . . .

And just before little brother got up to make his cards, as we were snuggling in the bed silently, as the words formed in my mouth and I was about to speak, he said to me, "I love you, too, Dad."

Yes, he said, I love you, too.

# Love is Open

On a cold morning, I sit with my hands folded together, conserving warmth.

*Open them.*

But what if conserving warmth isn't the best way to stay warm?

*Open them.*

What if huddling, hoarding, holding everything close and closed, tight and together, bundled and bound, isn't the best way to keep warm and to stop the cold from seeping in?

*Open them.*

In fact, what if keeping is entirely the wrong word?

*Open them.*

Keeping implies possession, scarcity, withholding.

*Open them.*

What if the best way to stay warm is to be warm?

*Open them.*

What if sharing our warmth, offering, extending, laying down our blanket and smoothing out our favorite corner for another, for all others, will make us warmer?

*Open them.*

And what if opening our hearts, letting our blood beat freely and fiercely, refusing to constrict the flow, is the best way to keep our hearts warm, too?

*Open them.*

A cold heart is perhaps the worst curse of all. I would rather suffer the loss of all I treasured than freeze my feelings, than allow my muscles of compassion to atrophy and heart callouses to form.

*Open them.*

You will feel it.

*Open them.*

The warmth.

*Open them.*

A different kind of warmth.

*Open them.*

A warmth drawn from an unquenchable fire, a warmth that radiates, a warmth that melts the ice of bitterness and burns away the residue of resentment, a warmth that resurrects the spirit. A warmth that rejuvenates the soul.

*Open them.*

*Open your hands.*

*Lay them out.*

*Palms up.*

*Accept love in the left one.*

*And tender kindness from the right.*

*Open them.*

*Open your hands.*

*And be warm today.*

*Be warm.*

# Love is Patience

Patience encompasses knowing, understanding, accepting, and embracing an evolved concept of change.

Patience is not putting up with what doesn't serve you, with what breaks you down and tears you apart instead of building you up and helping you become whole.

Patience is not resignation or blind acceptance of the *status quo*—that which remains the same and keeps us where we are.

Patience is the constant pursuit of *sursum corda*—that which lifts up our hearts and raises us to a higher place.

Patience is not Sisyphus pushing the rock up the hill each morning, Prometheus suffering as his liver is pecked away each day, Tantalus endlessly reaching up for the grapes, down for the water, never to touch either one, or tolerating cruelty and abuse. These are tortures and have nothing to do with patience.

Patience is knowing that change is messy, that transitions are not always crisp, that movement along the path takes time.

Patience is understanding that even when you get there, wherever you think your there is, you still need to be patient, because there is always another step to take if you choose to live a life that honors your feelings, a life in which you reach and grow.

Patience is Michelangelo.

Patience is his David.

Patience is the Sistine Chapel.

Michelangelo had the strength to pick up his chisel each day and chip away at the block of marble, to climb the scaffolding, raise his brush, and brighten the gesso with color.

Michelangelo had the patience to understand that art, the art of creating sculptures and frescoes, the art of living an inspired, purposeful, and fulfilling life, is not a means to an end but a process of transition.

Michelangelo had the wisdom to know that while his vision of what he wanted to realize was clear, the path to achieving that vision would take twists and turns—an unseen, internal flaw in the marble, a crack in the ceiling that wasn't there the day before—and he accepted that the path around these obstacles would be revealed as he moved farther along.

Michelangelo had the grace to know when to pause, to accept that completion is not perfection but part of an ongoing effort, that although an artist finishes individual works, there is only one work that is constantly in process—the work on the soul, the work of shaping, molding, and brightening the self in as close an approximation as possible to the image of the creator, an image we cannot see directly, only in reflection.

Michelangelo understood that freeing David from the marble was freeing himself to grow and change. He understood that the image preserved in the rock, the colors encased in the dried gesso of the ceiling, do not embody cessation of activity but bring to life each and every motion of the artist's hands and tools, and that these creations change all who experience them, each in a different way.

Michelangelo knew that patience is not standing still but active waiting.

## Love is Presence

It is no accident that presence and presents sound the same.

Presence is a gift.

We receive presence when another person is fully with us—body, mind, heart, and spirit—completely and unreservedly, and not partly somewhere else.

We give presence when we bring body, mind, heart, and spirit fully and freely, when we make nothing more important than being and living in the moment that is happening with another person.

We've all felt the magic of presence and the intense loss and disappointment of its absence, especially when the shell of the body is present, but the mind, heart, and spirit are not.

Presence is listening.

Presence is responding.

Presence is sharing.

Presence is joining.

Presence is accepting.

Presence is understanding.

Presence is embracing.

Presence is love.

Presence is gratitude.

Presence is pre-sense, meaning it precedes the senses. Before you can see, hear, smell, taste, or touch another, before you can enjoy all the wonders of that delicious, nourishing feast, you must bring yourself to the table, pull your chair up close, put your distractions, frustrations, resentments, judgments, and defensiveness away, and open yourself to the person who is before you, even if that person is you.

Withholding our presence from someone we love, consciously or not, unless it is to protect ourselves from harm and damage, is perhaps the most hurtful and destructive act we can commit in a relationship.

Giving our presence, even when all of life's demands clamor to pull us away, is perhaps the greatest gift we can give, not only to the person we love but also to ourselves.

When you look back, do you want to ask yourself, "Where was I?" or do you want to say, "I was there."

\* \* \*

There is irony in the title "Presence Revisited."

A need to return to a moment in which I was present but failed to absorb all I needed to learn, a need to go back to bring wisdom forward from present turned past to influence future. A need that surfaced yesterday, when I experienced an unfolding of moments that revealed secrets of presence I needed to understand.

It started when a friend reached out about clouds obscuring her sunny skies.

I have this friend because I am present, because I show up every day, share what I am learning, and show appreciation for what she and others like her share.

I reached back.

And we connected.

I reached back because I am receptive.

And I succeeded in helping because I listened, and listening is conducive to success.

Reflecting on why it worked, I realized that my presence with my friend was both connected and detached.

I connected with her and detached from my self,
from the parts of my self—resentment, frustration,
impatience—that could block connection had I not
worked to integrate them, through conscious practice,
into an evolving self, a self unbothered by intrusive
thoughts, uninfluenced by obtrusive needs, receptive
to the other and conducive to helping others see where
they need to be.

What I bring to the table are my talents and skills,
my ongoing spiritual education, my ability to make a
contribution using some powerful tools.

But my success depends not only on what but also on
who I bring to the table, my presence in each and every
interaction, who I am in the moment I connect with
another.

And if who I bring is clouded with unintegrated parts
of my self, my light is obscured, and the connection
disintegrates in darkness before it can begin.

The tapestry of moments continued unfolding when I
saw a tweet from Julie Daley quoting Peter Block from
his book *Stewardship*. "We are reluctant to let go of the
belief that if I am to care for something I must control
it." These words went to the heart of my dialogue
with my friend, my advice to let go a little, to guide
without directing, to lead without pushing, to allow the
other to find his or her own authority in speaking the
answers my friend already knew. I retweeted the quote,

which led Julie to my blog, and in turn, she shared my post "Over the Top" with her followers. One of them, in France, read it and retweeted, and we began a conversation. Of all things, my new friend Marion Chapsal writes about—and is set to give a speech on—presence. Her post helped me with the speech I am working on for my appearance at Make an Impact - Live! in Chicago—not with what I will bring to the podium, but with *who* I will bring, with how I will be present in the room, how I will detach from my self and connect with my audience. I fully believe these events, the texture and colors of the unfolded tapestry, are not random but meant to be, present by design.

And taking in the whole tapestry made me aware of the simple complexity of presence. When you practice it and achieve it, when you get it right, it becomes effortless, a way of being. But to get there requires a tremendous amount of complicated work.

Here are some thoughts on that work, on moving past intrusive and obtrusive presence, past the intrusive thoughts and obtrusive needs, to a state of receptive presence that is conducive to more effective interaction.

Embrace the other's imperfections as opportunities for improvement, their gaps in knowledge as openings for your wisdom, their stubbornness as evidence of their desperate need for your patient approach. If they were perfect, well-educated and enlightened, and fully open to transformation, they would not need you, and you know you have been called to help those who need precisely what you can provide.

Listen with full attention to their voices and do your best to silence your own until you have absorbed everything they are trying to convey. Even if they are lying, to themselves and you, there is a grain of truth, a kernel of meaning in what they're saying, and it's your job to strip away the husk and isolate that kernel. You may recognize the answer quickly, but you have to hold it, guard it even, until the other person is ready to hear it, or until through the skillful work of discovery you do with them, they come upon it themselves and speak it with their own authority.

When that happens, when the other person speaks with their authority the truth you have helped them discover, the truth on which you have shed the light that flows through you from the Creator of light, that truth becomes their own. And they can't live their truth, can't embrace it, can't wrap their mind, heart, and soul around it and start to feel its impact until they own it.

You can dispense advice worth millions, hold out the golden ticket, wave it frantically in front of their face. But that ticket is worthless unless they claim what's theirs and cash it in.

* * *

It is a miracle, how people we love become a part of us, a presence in yet separate from our selves, like threads of a different color woven into our soulcloth. In breakups and divorce, this cloth is ripped apart, and each injured partner must undertake the healing process of reweaving. A choice is made—whether to weave a new fabric, strong and tight, by pulling in, narrowing, and closing around the emptiness (the absence) and attempt to obliterate the presence of love and grief—or to incorporate new threads, to welcome love again, to push out, widen, and expand around the fullness (the presence) of love and risk, of suffering, and of true healing.

# Love is a Question

Yesterday, I set forth the four types of relationships in our lives that are the keys to achieving fulfillment and happiness: self, work, interpersonal, and spiritual.

Today, I'm advancing four questions to ask yourself about each of the four types of relationships in your life. Yes, that's a total of 16 questions, and some may be hard to answer honestly. But if you try, you just might find you (finally) get what you need.

The first question to ask is, "Does this relationship serve and support me?" This means, does the relationship make the hard parts of your life easier, take the edge off, lift you up when you're down, and fill your well with water, charge your batteries with energy? Or does it primarily serve the needs of another person or organization and contribute little or nothing to meeting your own needs?

The second question to ask is, "Does this relationship promote and improve my psychological health, or does it cause damage?" It is one thing for a partner, boss, or friend to hold us, constructively, to a higher standard of behavior and help us achieve it. It is another for someone to criticize us constantly, make us feel unloved, unappreciated, and unworthy, cause us to doubt ourselves, or demand that we sacrifice ourselves—our principles, our beliefs, our independence—to keep the peace in the relationship.

The third question to ask is, "Does this relationship enable me to grow and develop, or does it hold me back?" Are you constantly learning, and are your interests accepted and encouraged? Is the other party in the relationship a source of knowledge, wisdom, and perspective? Is your world expanding? Or is it shrinking, because you encounter strong, even overwhelming resistance to change and feel that if you try to push outside of the status quo you will be pushed back, perhaps brutally?

The fourth question to ask is the hardest. It has two parts. The first is, "What would my life be like if this relationship were different?" Answering this question requires you to suspend your disbelief for a moment and imagine that the relationship *could* be different, even if you feel the situation is hopeless. It may help to envision a different version of a person, your same boss having a different personality, a needy friend actually asking for once how you're doing. This can give you a taste of what change would look like and some needed perspective on the situation you are actually living. The second part of the question is even harder. "What would my life be like *without* this relationship?" This requires unconventional thinking and accepting the concept that absence creates presence, that no longer having a relationship that drains you, damages you, and holds you back, creates space in your life for relationships that support you, build up your health and well-being, and help you grow.

Asking and answering these questions about the first three types of relationships—self, work, and interpersonal—can bring about profound changes in your life.

Asking and answering them about the fourth type, the spiritual relationship, is more complicated. You may be with the right religion for you but in the wrong temple or church. You may not fully understand how your relationship with God, if you have one, serves you. You may feel forsaken or see the higher power as an angry presence, not a loving one. You may feel bound and limited by a belief set that in your heart you do not accept. These are personal matters for each of us. But no matter what your beliefs, you can try to be open to a relationship with spirituality that serves and supports you, promotes your psychological health, and enables you to learn and grow.

\* \* \*

Some of us have been with people and through experiences that have caused us to ask, "Am I unlovable? Is there something about me that just cannot be loved?"

Does my very being engender hatred, scorn, contempt, abuse, withdrawal of emotional support and affection, withholding of attention and love? Is it me, God, is it me? Do I deserve this shit? What on earth am I doing wrong?"

Unless you are by nature cruel, spiteful, mean-spirited, vindictive, stingy with your own gifts, unappreciative of others' efforts and generosity, I can assure you, it isn't you.

I'll say that again. It isn't you.

And I suspect, if you've asked yourself the unlovable question, that you're none of the things I just mentioned. That you are, in fact, the opposite: kind and loving, understanding, compassionate, forgiving, generous, and accommodating to the point of sacrificing your self.

The only aspect of your situation that's in your control is the choices you've made and continue to make—the unhealthy people you choose to be around (such as dysfunctional partners and abusive bosses), the way you allow those you have to be around (family) to treat you, and the false hope you maintain that if you love these people just a little bit more, they'll change their unhealthy behavior.

We're wired to embrace change when it suits us and serves us and to resist it when it suits others and requires effort.

It takes a leap of faith, and trust in God's direction, to take on the hard work of being the best we can be for another without sacrificing ourselves, and we can only do this when our effort is appreciated and returned.

If you've asked yourself the unlovable question, you're probably around people who love you as long as you do what they want and dump on you and try to shame or manipulate you when you don't.

These people may claim to love you. But they don't respect you. And respect is an essential quality of love.

First, find your security in God's love, which He offers freely to all.

Then, respect yourself and require respect from others as the price of walking through your door, the ticket to boarding your soul train, the key to unlocking your chest of treasures.

If you consistently give yourself away, or let people take as much as they want without giving in return or showing appreciation, no one will value you.

Set a firm, non-negotiable price, saying to yourself, I am worth it. I am worthy.

And if you feel unlovable, remember, it's not you or what you're offering.

It's the blindness of others to your lovability.

It's their own sad inability to love.

It isn't you, my friend.

It isn't you.

## Love is Reconciliation

Most people think of reconciliation as giving in to another person's demands, losing autonomy, sacrificing a cherished principle for the sake of forced peace. But that type of resolution is not true reconciliation; it is detente, a tense stalemate held in place only by the threat of mutually assured destruction.

True reconciliation includes and is defined by forgiveness. In addition to making peace with the other person, we must also make peace with our own anger and negativity and stop clinging to the past as proof of the other person's mean spirit, stubborn wrongheadedness, and fault for the entire mess.

Clinging to the past is not processing it and learning from it. It's pulling past into present, and it prevents us from living in, enjoying, and appreciating the present moment and all it has to offer.

Here are two examples to illustrate the point. The first comes from my professional life. I worked for many years in sales, and no good salesperson gets credit or advances by repeating, "Hey, remember that quarter five years ago when I beat the numbers?" Your past successes are your past successes, and leaving them behind gives you the freedom to leave your past failures back there with them and focus on present accomplishments and planning for the future.

The other example comes from the past. I knew a man once, a hardcore Red Sox fan, who loved to listen to baseball games. In the late 1980s, after Sony had come out with the Walkman and replaced the ill-fitting single earpiece with comfortable stereo headphones, this man still listened to those games on an ancient transistor radio in a worn leather case, clapped hard against one ear. The radio may have had a sentimental association for him, but it struck me that by clinging to that obsolete radio and its poor sound quality, he was unconsciously sacrificing his enjoyment of his beloved baseball games.

Too many people think that they will lose too much— their pride, the respect of others, their self-respect—by reconciling, particularly if the estranged parties are family members. Positions become hardened over time, fortifications and defenses are built and expanded, and with each passing day, month, and year, it becomes more difficult to tear these down and let the other person in, because you've invested (wasted) so much time and energy keeping the other person out.

The effort expended here is akin to what the financial world calls sunk costs—money you've put in and are never going to get back. But in the emotional world, you can recover your investment and multiply it many times, turning loss into gain by giving the gift of true reconciliation and forgiveness.

The peace dividend—losing the cost of maintaining those walls, turrets, missile silos, and satellite shields—pays handsomely, and you will find yourself suddenly free to share your new-found wealth, not only with the person you've reconciled with, but with others in your life whom you've been ignoring, shutting out, or even refusing to see as a form of punishment for the other person or because they took the other person's side.

The part of our brain that thinks we are giving in and losing if we reconcile is a primitive part. It thrives on the stuff that lives in the primeval muck—hubris, vengeance, stoicism, and most of all, fear. Our fear of loss, particularly if we've suffered severe losses earlier in our lives, such as the loss of a parent at a young age, learning we were adopted, loss of fertility before having children, or loss of an essential physical function, overwhelms us, and we cling to the way of being we've developed to be able to cope with, to be able to bear these losses and go on with our lives.

But we lose so much more by clinging to our unhealthy behaviors and closing off worlds of possibility, forgoing moments of joy and elation, and blaming others for our self-induced misery.

Reconciliation and forgiveness can't erase the past— your own past losses and hurts or the hurts you and another person may have visited on each other. But it can put the past in perspective, and like the first two-point perspective drawing you did in art class, the one with the road vanishing into the distance, it puts you at the other end of that road, the far end, walking, then breaking into a run towards someone you love, have always loved. Life is short, and the road ends for all of us at some point.

It takes all the aspects of aplomb—strength, patience, wisdom, and especially grace—to give the rewarding gift of reconciliation. It's not easy, but it's worth it. Do it, before you find it's too late.

# Love is Sanctuary

There are times in our life when we need sanctuary.

Safety.

Refuge.

Protection.

From others and from ourselves.

We need sanctuary when we are hurt, when we are weak, when we are fallen, when we are grieving.

A closed place with an open-ended commitment to revelation and healing.

A walled garden where we can tear down our walls and let the light in so growth can begin again.

A place free of judgment, where fears can be shared without fear, where tears can flow without shame or embarrassment, where slings and arrows fly by harmlessly as we remove our bandages and open our wounds to the air.

One definition of sanctuary is "a consecrated place where sacred objects are kept." Consecrated means "solemnly dedicated to or set apart for a high purpose."

The sacred object is the self.

The high purpose is restoration.

The hardest times in life are when the place that has been our sanctuary, the person whose embrace has sheltered us, no longer serves. These changes may be temporary or permanent, and at first, it can be hard to tell. Stress can render a person unable to provide what he once did, and calm has the potential to restore the ability to give. But people also change, or put another way, they crack, and we may discover when they hit their fault lines that they are not entirely who we believed and wanted them to be. And of course, death can take a person's physical presence, though it cannot steal the sanctuary a special person gave us while here.

When you need your sanctuary, you will find it. Or it will find you, perhaps unexpectedly.

It can be frightening to enter at first. The self shrinks a little, as you are overcome with gratitude, as you feel the higher purpose taking over. And then you remember, "I have been here before." You may not be in the same place, the same embrace, but yes, yes, you have been there before. The place on your map you can find with your eyes closed.

# Love is Shelter

There are times in our lives when we are compelled to seek shelter and times when we are called to provide it.

Shelter is more than a place, a roof over our head, a safe spot to stay for a while.

Shelter is a commitment to protect.

When your college roommate visits for a few days, you may provide a bed, some meals, and entertainment. But you are not providing shelter.

When a runaway shows up at your door, you take responsibility for a foster child, or you open your heart and your home to a friend in need, you are providing shelter.

The ability to provide shelter requires four qualities: Love, Compassion, Courage, and Generosity.

Love opens the heart to understanding and appreciating the other person's need for shelter.

Compassion gives us the impetus to take action and make the offer or accept the request.

Courage enables us to assume the risk of providing shelter, for we may be protecting someone from dark forces or self-disintegration.

Generosity frees us to use all our available resources and give abundantly to fulfill the call.

And as we round the circle, the ultimate protection, the protection of love, flows through all four spaces.

# Love is Sweet

Usually, the title of the post comes first.

I type it in the box up there, having already distilled the rich flavor of the words that will flow below before pouring the first drop into the cup.

An enticing whiff of aromatic steam.

But not today.

Today I'm doing it backward.

This morning, my younger son got up, wrapped in all his blankets, and took his usual place on the chaise in the living room. I had started to make breakfast and went over to say good morning and give him a hug. As I held him in my arms, kissing his forehead, I said, "Are you sweet?"

"Yes."

"Yes, you are sweet," I said, holding him tighter, feeling him wiggle to break free of my embrace.

"I'm loving sweet, but I'm not sugar sweet."

He is five.

And with the simplicity of a child, he unpacked the complexity of a word.

He unfolded sweetness for me.

He showed me giving sweet without taking sweet.

He showed me heart sweet without mouth sweet.

He showed me eternal sweet without temporal, momentary sweet.

And he gave me the title for today's post.

Sweet, right?

* * *

I woke late this morning, too late to make coffee to take to work with me, despite the patient insistence of my beeping clock.

Without coffee to drink before leaving for the train or pour into my commuter mug, I decided to stop at the gourmet coffee and pastry shop across from the station. I ordered a large skim latte, and I was bowled over with the first sip.

This latte was special.

It was rich, not too sweet, luscious in texture, and full of the alchemy that occurs when freshly roasted coffee combines with scalded—not burnt—milk.

I drank it lustfully, standing on the cold platform, sipping my hot cup of happiness.

And when I thought I had finished it, I walked towards the trash bin to throw it away. But before I did, I opened the cup.

And lo and behold, the foam!

The thought that I might have tossed the cup in the garbage without enjoying, without indulging in the glorious color, taste, and texture of the magical air-milk mixture at the bottom was a frightful one.

I extended my tongue as far as I could into the cup to lap it up.

I tipped and tapped to bring the foam closer to my lips. And still, there was a substantial amount of it clinging to the bottom. I was determined to get it all.

I tried tearing the rim, but it was too well-constructed. So I took out my house key, drove it through the side of the cup, and pulled up through the rim to open it wide. And I buried my face in it. Yum!

I didn't care what my fellow commuters, some of whom were staring, thought. If they had *this* foam in their cups, they would want to do the same thing, I was sure of it. So I kept at it.

Sated at last, I parted with the cup and wiped my foam-covered face with my handkerchief.

And I was happy, because I had drunk every last drop of the elixir, dug to the bottom to unearth the buried treasure.

I had found the love at the bottom of my cup.

# Love is Tender

*Seems like without tenderness there's something missing*
*Tenderness*
*Where is the*
*Tenderness*
*Where is it?*

*Tenderness* — General Public

Before I write, I listen.

I listen for words in the silence.

Silence is not empty.

Silence is full of words . . . if you listen.

This morning I heard a word . . . tenderness.

After I listen, I look for signs.

Signs are everywhere . . . if you look for them.

And this morning I saw a sign, on the platform: an old man, standing behind a woman who was, if not his wife, his companion through a long stretch of time.

The man's hair was wispy and gray, his face weathered. He had the weariness of age but not the slackness of resignation. He was flush with the life force still in him.

The woman was slightly taller, broad in the shoulders and broader still in the hips, her hair coiffed and dyed an attractive shade of blonde.

At the moment I passed them, the man leaned in, craned his neck upward a bit, paused briefly with a potent mix of respect and appreciation for the woman's space and beauty, placed his hands gently on her shoulders, and pressed his lips into her hair, onto her nape.

There was passion in his kiss.

Passion and pleasure.

I could see him savoring it.

Passion and pleasure tempered with tenderness.

The raw metals of love alloyed with the magical ore mined from his heart to render this man soft *and* strong.

The look on his face as he kissed her was blissful.

His eyes were closed, his cheeks alight with the explosive fire of memory stoked by imagination.

His body, shrunken with age, stretched to reach a spot crossed many times on their journey together, to brush his lips there with evident delight, the way a painter smiles as his brushstrokes bring color, light, and life to a canvas.

And in that stretching lies the root of tenderness, for the root word *ten* means stretch.

Tenderness requires stretching.

Tenderness is something we extend.

Tenderness enlarges a gesture, expands a statement, transforms a relationship from ordinary to extraordinary, filling it with softness that makes it strong.

Stretching requires effort, commitment, patience, and flexibility.

It helps to exercise your tenderness muscle, your tendon of tenderness, every day.

Because the work of tenderness is never done.

And the joy of tenderness is never-ending.

\* \* \*

# The Alphabet of Love

In tenderness there is wisdom.

And in wisdom there is tenderness.

The wisdom of knowing that life without tenderness, without both giving and receiving it, is incomplete.

And the tenderness of knowing when someone you love needs wisdom, and knowing when that person needs nothing more than a smile, a hot cup of tea, a listening ear, the soft brush of the back of your hand against her hair, or even to be left alone and have his need for solitude respected.

To me, tender acts are not acts of delicacy and softness. They are acts of courage and resolve. They are acts that recognize the delicacy and softness of others, acts that flow from knowing we are all soft, easily injured, and delicate in places, some obvious and some not.

Acts that presuppose the purpose of our presence here is easing suffering.

Acts that by example engender tenderness in others.

Acts that stretch but do not break our boundaries.

Acts that place the need for love at the center of our common humanity.

Acts of selfless extension where cost is not weighed because benefit sits on a different scale.

Acts of being there when needed most.

Acts of graceful withdrawal.

Acts commanded and blessed by the spirit that breathes within us.

Acts that cause us to delve deeper into our hearts than we believed possible.

Acts that enable us, ever so briefly, to touch the stars.

## Love is Tone

In the second I had to sit in my space today I felt the word tone.

I say felt, because I didn't hear the word.

I sensed it as I marveled at the warm glow of morning light brightening the red and green leaves outside my window, suffusing them with color, intensifying the richness of their hues.

Just as I might have felt the cold, flat, foreboding tone of a densely clouded sky and the impending fall of rain.

We think of tone as auditory, a musical term or a reference to tone of voice.

But we feel a tone when someone speaks to us.

Feel it in our bones.

We feel whether the person speaking holds love and respect or hatred and contempt for us in the heart.

Tone goes beyond sound, capturing—and reflecting—the mood, spirit, quality, manner, character, and atmosphere that a person, place, object, or work of art creates, as well as "the particular quality of brightness, deepness, or hue of a tint or shade of a color."

It's the particular quality that interests me.

A particular quality of brightness is brilliance.

A particular quality of deepness is wisdom.

A particular quality of hue creates a color—or a personality—that is displeasing or pleasing, clashing or complementary.

A leader sets the tone for a meeting or an entire enterprise—energized and productive, supportive and understanding, cold and unforgiving, cynical and hopeless.

A photographer adjusts, emphasizes, and enhances tones in pictures—warm and inviting, severe and stark, dark and moody—either through fine-tuning the mix of chemicals or the magic of digital alteration.

A conductor sets the tone for a passage of music—lively and spirited, morose and melancholy, aggressive and impatient, relaxed and easygoing.

And partners in a relationship set the tone for love.

More accurately, it is usually one partner, the one whose mood tends to dominate, who sets the tone for conversation (or argument), cooperation (or lack thereof), and lovemaking (or sex without love).

And we know a tone when we feel it.

The words may say one thing: "I love you. You mean everything to me. I can't live without you."

But the tone of everyday interaction reveals the truth.

Is it soothing?

Does it make your soul sing?

Or does it grate against your very being?

Is it warm like a well-stoked fire, or cold like a night wind that blows out every candle you try to light?

Is it happy, like a childhood photograph catching you by surprise in a moment of mirth, or forced like the cheesy smile you put on for the camera?

Is it sonorous or discordant?

Biting or considerate?

Loving or trying to sound like love?

Tone will always tell you everything you need to know.

## Love is Understanding

Death, the universal inevitable, is barely understood.

Science monitors the signs of life, and history records the time of their cessation.

There is breath and then, there is no breath.

The doctor says, "I'm sorry," and moves on.

Time now exists for us in terms of before and after.

But what happens in the moment remains a mystery.

There is a tear in the fabric.

A flap opens.

The departing spirit escapes as it closes, leaving a perfect surface and an invisible scar that only the bereaved can feel.

# The Alphabet of Love

The tear on the surface disappears.

But the mirror tear, the one inside the heart, does not.

The change in the living brought on by the change in the dead remains.

We bury the body, fill the grave with dirt, but the gaping hole, the grievous wound, remains open.

Open and raw.

Deepened by shallow thoughts.

Widened by narrow-minded platitudes.

Caved in by the sudden avalanche of memory.

Absorbing tears the way water sinks into beach sand as a child pours from her bucket.

And the hole never quite closes.

We stitch it up, as best we can, eager to feel whole again.

But the moment we do start to feel whole again, we finger the jagged, bumpy scar with perverse curiosity until it throbs, overcome by the guilt of forgetting fused with the need to remember.

Pain cannot be buried in a box or sealed in an urn.

It must be taken out every so often, so we can feel its weight, its heft in our hands, its sharp contours that cut to the bone.

Acknowledging the suffering, refusing its denial, and embracing the excruciating growth it brings, is the only way to hold on to the joy the pain took from us, to carry it forward, and to be free to create joy in our remaining moments, knowing, that at any moment, we may lose that joy again.

# Love is Vigilant

In Greek mythology, the owl was considered a protector and the favorite bird of Athena, goddess of wisdom.

Here's what I find interesting about owls.

Their vision is both compromised and enhanced. First, they are farsighted and cannot see things right in front of them. Second, their eyes are fixed in their sockets. Imagine if you couldn't move your eyes from side to side.

And yet, owls are among the most effective seers and predators. One reason is their excellent nocturnal vision. Another is their ability to swivel their heads 270 degrees. This swiveling enables owls to see what's behind them without facing their bodies in a backward direction. It also allows them to turn until they can hear a sound with both ears simultaneously, helping them pinpoint their prey's exact location.

A protector looks for threats in every direction.

Threats from the past, threats in the present, threats possible in the future.

Threats around the 270-degree arc of time.

A protector also sees invisible threats, threats that lie in darkness, in the hidden quadrant, on the last 90 degrees of the circle.

A protector is vigilant.

And vigilant was the word that came to me this morning, along with the image of the owl.

We all need owls in our lives, those vigilant people who protect us not only from what we cannot see but also from what they cannot see but only sense.

Who is your owl?

## Love is Vast

Nearly all of us have felt the falling, the risky backwards dive into the crazy abyss, the pleasant drowning under the overwhelming flood of feeling, the sinking against which we put up no struggle, the moment of time when everything becomes immeasurable, the rapture, the bliss. There is a reason we call it *falling* in love.

But after the fall, when you enter love, when you fully allow love to enter and inhabit you, the motion of descent falls away.

Love . . . floats.

You are on your back, looking up at a cloudless blue sky, held up by your heart's buoyancy, supported and sustained by a vast ocean of tenderness, rocking gently in the peaceful waves. You can relax, because love has your back. Love is under you, surrounding you, carrying you, keeping you afloat on your journey.

Love's waters run deep, and they hold countless buried treasures and undiscovered secrets. There are shipwrecks in these seas, but there are also many proud vessels, their tall masts reaching skyward, white sails unfurled to catch the breath of wind, their strong, stable anchors ready to be lowered at the shore.

The physics of floating involves displacement, and love displaces fear, loneliness, anguish, and unforgiveness. Love also displaces bitterness, for love is sweet.

Love feels fresh and yet familiar. We have floated in this water, but we cannot remember when. And love carries an eternal quality, because its source is the infinite One, the One who created love, the One who *is* love.

If love is like the buoyant saltwater of the ocean, then perhaps love is . . . God's tears.

## Love is Wondrous

Have you lost your sense of wonder?

Over time, through experience, much of it painful, we become jaded and cynical. We begin to think we've seen it all, to resign ourselves to the idea that nothing can be tried that hasn't been tried before, and to view hope as the opiate of the deluded.

We've all been to this desolate, lifeless place at least once in our lives. But the land of the lost is not a place; it's a state of mind. And that means you can change it.

Go out and experience nature. Marvel at the confluence of its utter randomness and exquisite organization.

Look at a picture of a newborn child—those tiny fingers and wrinkly skin—an unpredictable bundle of potential.

Watch some footage of an athlete at the top of his or her game—Nadia Comaneci or Mary Lou Retton in the Olympics, Gale Sayers or Walter Payton running for the Bears—and let yourself be amazed by their talent, dedication, and perfect execution.

Visit a museum, and stare at masterpieces for hours.

Call a friend—the one who's stuck with you through everything—and appreciate the miracle of human loyalty.

Silence the voice that wants to say, "So what?" to these things. They are, indeed, amazing.

Let your eyes go wide with wonder.

Take in the unexpected, the inexplicable.

Suspend your disbelief.

Hang your disbelief from the rafters and choke it until it is good and dead.

And let the wonder in.

## Love is Exquisite

We live for exquisite moments.

We often say we would die for them.

Before they occur, we fantasize about them, often fed by images of popular culture, and after they've passed, we enshrine them in memory, retelling, reliving, clutching at the faintest hint of their fullness, constantly trying to recreate their magic.

We often believe these moments to be fortunate accidents.

Happenstance.

A kind of manna from heaven.

And God *was* present, but not in the way we think.

We look back at exquisite moments as re-presentations of possibility.

The embodiment of hope—the hope of finding things long lost.

We cradle them carefully, hold them to our hollows like a child.

We hallow them as sacred and inscribe them in our book of life, turning to those lines again and again that serve as bright breaks from the dark accumulated tedium, those bursts of flight that lift us temporarily from gravity's endless drag, the exclamation points that punctuate the passage of time to which we've been sentenced.

We treat them no differently than tragic blows, stumbling through the aftermath, unable to solve the equation, awestruck, wondering, how could this have happened?

How did everything align to create an alchemical reaction whose recipe is now forgotten?

We scramble to repeat the sequence of symbols, to find the list of what we threw into the fire, inevitably failing to forge our own bliss.

The bliss that lives inside us.

The bliss we've already been given.

Exquisite moments are not brought about by anything external.

They do not depend on the perfect ingredients or any ingredients at all.

They come when we are ready to receive them, when we open ourselves, when we strip away the feelings, frustrations, falsehoods, and fables that corrupt our true substance, when we arrive bare, naked, humble, and real.

They never come when we try to force them.

They come, instead, when we seek them.

Exquisite has come to mean uniquely splendid, but its original meaning is "carefully sought out."

And to seek the exquisite, we must first give ourselves permission to go on the quest.

We must tell ourselves it is not only OK but also our right to be happy, loved, fulfilled, and accepted.

And we must seek the One who accepts us as we are.

To hallow is to make holy, and to transform a moment from ordinary to exquisite, from mundane to holy, we must seek God and allow Him in, hallow Him in, hallow and allow Him to inhabit the moment with us, to inhabit *us* in the moment.

For it is doing this that prepares us for the most exquisite moment of all—the moment of ultimate acceptance.

## Love is Yellow
## (and every other color)

I came to gardening late in life, though it was a passion
of my father's.

I appreciated the beauty but resented the work.

I loved looking through bulb catalogs with my mother,
from places with names like Touch of Holland and
Dutch Delight, ordering dozens of tulips in red, orange,
yellow, and midnight black, adding in variegated
varieties and even some with their edges fringed.

I enjoyed mapping out diagrams of where each group
would go in our yard—a circle here, a figure-eight there,
a line of color to offset the green bushes behind a bed.

But when the bulbs came, all neatly labeled in their
cardboard boxes and burlap bags and it was time to
plant them, time to take the digger from its hook in the
garage and get my hands dirty, I resisted, forcing my

mother to nag and eventually kick me into action, just as she did with the papers I had to write for school.

After I did the planting, I felt a sense of accomplishment and anticipation. I hoped the squirrels wouldn't dig the bulbs up for a snack. I waited expectantly for the green shoots to burst through the black ground, the stalks to rise steadily, the elliptical buds to form, and the bright flowers to finally unfurl as if to say, "Here I am! Look at me! I've come to bring you joy!"

This morning, taking an early walk in my garden, I noticed the onset of the spring weed invasion— dandelions and other unwanteds cropping up to consume precious nutrients, threatening to crowd out what I've planted on purpose.

As I've come to care more actively for my garden, to do it without being nagged and kicked, to embrace the work of tending and nurturing, to enjoy it, and to embed the practice of clearing into my routine, I've learned something about weeding.

It's easiest to pull weeds in the morning, when the soil is still damp and before sunlight hits. At this time of day, the weeds slide right out, roots and all, when I pull them, while later, they cling to the dirt stubbornly—the tops snap off but the roots remain.

I'm sure there's a good explanation for this, but I don't need to research it.

I understand it—all too well.

Now is the season to care for my garden. To protect it and keep it free of weeds. To shower my love on my favorite plants. To protect them from what would harm them. To tend and nurture and oversee their growth. To be the one who helps them blossom and grace the world with their blooms.

\* \* \*

I'm not sure

If this year's leaves—

The spoils of fall from summer plundered—

Have multiplied in glory greater

Than ever I recall . . .

Or if,

Perhaps,

It's only

My newly minted eyes,

Witnessing the season's riches,

Observing their increase.

# The Alphabet of Love

Coins golden on the boughs of the realm,

A currency held close and tight,

Before they drop, spent,

Dying to buy my breathtaking moments of orange and yellow, russet and red,

Their purchase ransoming the removal of warmth,

Expending themselves in the ultimate sacrifice,

Brightening the dark descent into winter,

Redeeming the dreary days,

Before their treasure corrodes and crumbles,

Then blows away like dust in the wind.

I'm not sure, but I know this . . .

I know I am grateful,

For everything given,

For everything sacrificed,

For everything redeemed.

I am grateful for all of it—

For every last and fast falling leaf,

Grateful for God's most precious gift—

Grateful.

# Love is Zeal

Do what you love.

Pursue your passion.

Let your light shine.

Wise words from those who've won the battle against the baser self, the self that treads water but never learns to swim, the self that is exposed to light but never develops, the self that takes refuge in the dark boredom of getting by instead of standing triumphant atop the bright citadel of dreams.

These people make it look both hard and easy.

They struggled, of course, for struggle is ever-present.

They pushed past resistance, ignored criticism, overcame obstacles, and made it happen.

They broke through, to the other side.

A door was shown to them, an open door in the distance. A door whose appealing shape and proportions pleased them, a door whose light drew them closer, a door in the sky, a door to the stars, those miraculous bursts of brightness stretched toward us on beams of traveling light.

Are the stars finite?

Could you ever count them all?

Is there not a star for every one of us . . . and more?

There is only one secret in all the books and blogs successful people have written, all the tapes and videos they've made and lectures they've given, all the coaching they've provided, all the advice they've ever offered.

And that secret is no secret at all.

The door they walked through has been given to each of us, to all of us, a universal gift.

It is our door.

It is ardor.

Ardor is flame, fire, burning, heat.

Ardor is eagerness and zeal.

Ardor is not the consumption of burning.

Ardor is the glow.

The association of flame, fire, and burning with that place we don't want to end up is meant to confuse us. That place is actually a place of cold and darkness, where warmth is absent, where light never shines. There is consumption there, constant consumption and depletion. And there is no glow. Only shadows.

In the other place, the place of light, there is constant creation, endless regeneration, constant burning of the same eternal energy we've been given, spirited fanning of the flame sparked within us, and an infinitely golden glow.

We were created to create.

We were born to burn brightly.

Each in our own way.

Our door is ardor.

Ardor is our door.

Given to you with love,

Tom

Made in the USA
Monee, IL
26 May 2022

97061354R00079